A Helping Hand

Your guide to hiring and working with a lawyer during compensation claims

Lisa Rennie

A Helping Hand: Your guide to hiring and working with a lawyer during compensation claims © Lisa Rennie, 2021

www.lisarennie.com

The moral rights of Lisa Rennie to be identified as the author of this work have been asserted in accordance with the Copyright Act 1968

First published in Australia 2021 by Lisa Rennie.

ISBN 978-0-6453707-0-6

All rights reserved. No part of this publication may be reproduced or transmitted by any means, electronic, photocopying or otherwise, without prior written permission of the author.

Disclaimer

All the information, techniques, skills and concepts contained within this publication are of the nature of general comment only and are not in any way recommended as individual advice. The intent is to offer a variety of information to provide a wider range of choices now and in the future, recognising that we all have widely diverse circumstances and viewpoints. Every reader should choose to make use of the information herein. This is their decision, and the author and publishers do not assume any responsibilities whatsoever under any conditions or circumstances. The author does not take responsibility for the business, financial, personal or other success, results or fulfilment upon the readers' decision to use this information. It is recommended that the reader obtain their own independent advice.

Disclaimer

Nothing in this book is intended to be or to replace legal advice.

This is a guidebook to hiring and working with a lawyer.

You should seek independent legal advice as soon as possible in relation to your specific circumstances as important time limits may apply.

This is really important, read this page again!

Dedicated to Mrs May Donoghue

Preface

It was 1986 and I was in my final year of primary school. I had waited over a month for our last project to be marked. The teacher asked a classmate, Todd, if his work was ready to hand in and again, it wasn't. She said he could have another week to complete it, otherwise she would start to deduct marks. She wasn't marking any of the work until everyone had handed in their work. Out of nowhere I said with a slight tremble in my voice, "But that's not fair, if we all had an extra five weeks, imagine what more we could have done on our projects."

I think that a strong sense of what is fair is what lead me to being a lawyer and, in particular, to work in the area of personal injury law. As a side note, as an adult, I can now recognise that we don't know what was going on in Todd's life at the time. Todd, if you are reading this, my apologies that 12-year-old Lisa didn't have the skills to enquire what might have been going on in your 12-year-old life at that time.

I was fortunate to have parents who valued education and who always encouraged me to go after whatever it was that I wanted to achieve. When it came time for a week of work experience in High School, I had no idea what I wanted to do but then I suppose, not many 15-year-olds do. I considered doing a week of work at a cinema or a theme park but my mum encouraged me to apply for a place at the local Magistrates Court. In that week at the local courthouse, while I worked my way through mountains of mail, I saw lawyers who were proud of their work. They believed in what they were doing for their clients, and something about that stuck with me.

When it came time for me to apply for University, I applied for a business degree. This was partly because my mum was encouraging me to apply for law. Here's a tip to any parents reading this: - your children might resist what you want or what you think is best. If they do, my suggestion is to let them think it's their idea if you want it to happen.

In my early 20s after graduating with a Bachelor of Business, I realised that I was capable of completing a Law degree, and it was here that I would embark upon an almost 20-year career working in the legal industry. I studied at night and I worked in a law firm during the day. I realised quickly that I enjoyed acting for real people (not companies). I would get to learn their story and help them through a significantly hard and uncertain time of their lives. Again, I was guided by that sense of fairness and I was focussed on recovering compensation to put them back in the position that they would have been if the accident had not happened. Everyone had an individual story to tell and what might appear as a common injury could have such a wide and varying impact on different people and those around them.

The legal industry was good to me. I worked hard and I made the most of all the opportunities I was given. I worked in the personal injury field for almost 20 years. In that time, I did my training as a lawyer, acted for many injured people and in later years I worked as the General Manager for one of Queensland's leading personal injury firms. Now, it is a time that I look back on with pride, gratitude and mostly smiles.

After almost 20 years, my time in law was done and now it is a time where I can try new things, which I am so grateful to be able to do. But, all those client conversations over the years, the experiences and the knowledge, it seems wrong to just suddenly stop and that not be used in any way. That is what has led me to put pen to paper, so to speak, and writing this book is a way of sharing my knowledge and paying respect to past clients, mentors, and colleagues who taught me so much along that journey.

My hope is that by writing this book and sharing my views, based on my observations and experience, the readers of this book can gain a sense of comfort and avoid sleepless nights worrying about things that they need to not worry about. Sometimes we all need someone to tell us how we are feeling or what we are experiencing is something that most people feel or experience and we have comfort that we are not alone and are on the right path.

Table of Contents

Preface ix

Introduction 1

Chapter 1: But I'm not one of those people 11

Chapter 2: How to pick a lawyer 23

Chapter 3: Signing a costs agreement 37

Chapter 4: Keeping costs down 45

Chapter 5: Can I change lawyers? 57

Chapter 6: Why is the claim taking so long? 67

Chapter 7: "But my friend said…" 75

Chapter 8: Settling out of court 83

Chapter 9: What happens once we settle? 91

Real-Life Stories 96

Conclusion 119

Special people 122

About The Author 125

Introduction

I guess that you have picked up this book because you have, or someone you love has, suffered an injury and you have either engaged a lawyer to act on your behalf or you are working out if the legal path is one which you want to take and if you do, which lawyer will you pick?

Life after an injury raises all sorts of uncertainty. Recovering from an injury creates uncertainty around whether you will ever recover 100%, whether your sick leave will run out, how will the rent or mortgage get paid, will you ever get back to your job and then there is the impact on the loved ones around you to manage and that fear that they might just move on without you. These are common fears and concerns that I would have clients express to me almost daily. Uncertainty can be one of the most difficult things for people to manage.

There are doctors and therapists who help with the injury and lawyers can help advise and guide you through the legal process. For many people who have never been through this process and they have never worked with a lawyer before, it can feel like an extra stress and another new thing to deal with and to manage even though the lawyer is there to make your life easier.

Dealing with lawyers, the legal process, your injury and the associated stress can be a challenge. My goal here is to help you through the process.

This book is not intended to replace legal advice, in fact, you will have such specific and unique circumstances that I would recommend you get a lawyer to give you specific advice as soon as possible. That was really important, so I will say it again, I recommend you contact a lawyer to discuss your options and to know all specific deadlines relating to you, as soon as possible.

This book is written to help you to find the right lawyer for you and your circumstances, to help you to identify if your lawyer is doing a good job, to save you unknowingly inflating your own legal fees and to offer some reassurance and give you peace of mind.

For people who engage a lawyer and make a claim for compensation, it is not uncommon to feel like there is a process going on but maybe you got forgotten in the process. Sometimes you will find yourself questioning if your lawyer is really listening, if they have a heart and questioning what is happening and why. Here's the thing: lawyers do what they do every day, so it becomes normal for them. It doesn't make them bad lawyers. In fact, they are probably very good at what they do. They just forget that this isn't an everyday process for you and that it is your life and future they are talking about. Sometimes they are so busy getting the job done for you and, because they know there is nothing to worry about, they forget that you don't necessarily know that too.

During my time in law, the same questions and concerns came up time and time again. Maybe they are questions you have had, maybe they are questions that will arise in the future. I am here to give you piece of mind on those things.

I am not working as a lawyer now. That chapter is closed for me, but as a final legacy project, I decided to share my experience in this book and I hope it will ease your mind. I hope this book will assist you picking the right lawyer for your circumstances, help you see if your lawyer is doing a good job, and ultimately save you both money and unnecessary sleepless nights.

Every time you are feeling uneasy, pick this book up and find the chapter that relates to where you are at. Maybe I am telling you exactly what your lawyer is saying, and it will ease your mind – or maybe not, but then you will know if it is time to ask further questions.

Often someone who is injured is in no state physically or mentally to consider anything else, other than just focusing on their recovery, which is totally understandable. That can often leave a spouse or a loved one to be the main contact for lawyers. That can feel like a big responsibility for that person. It is human nature that we seem to do a better job for others than we do for ourselves.

So not only is the spouse or loved one left dealing with an injured person, worrying about the future but they can also feel the extra pressure of wanting to make the best decisions when it comes to guiding any dealings with lawyers and all the decisions involved with that. But regardless of whether it is you that is injured or a loved one, this book is absolutely for you.

It might not feel like this stage of your life will ever be over and that brighter days are ahead. I can assure you that one day the dealings with lawyers will come to an end, and the uncertainty you face right now will be only a memory and you will be in a new phase of life. I can't guarantee what that will look like, but life will go on and the overwhelm that you face right now will pass.

I have included a chapter of stories from people like you, people who were injured and went through the claims process with a lawyer. You might relate to different parts of each story, but what is common to each of them is that it is all in the past for them now, they have been where you are right now, and now they are through it and want you to learn from their experiences too. They were all extremely generous in sharing their stories and they wished there was a book like this when they were where you are now. They hoped for something just to give them some sort of assurance to help them trust the lawyer they picked, that how they felt was normal and that maybe some things they were worrying about were unnecessary.

Think of this like a guidebook to working with your lawyer. Imagine you were at a barbeque and met a friendly personal injury lawyer. Think of all the questions you would ask them about your lawyer and case and how much better you would feel knowing what was worth worrying about and what wasn't. Well, we might meet at a barbeque one day, but just in case we don't, you have this book instead.

Glossary (Words that lawyers use and what they really mean)

Lawyers use language that is everyday to them and maybe not for you. You should never be afraid or embarrassed to ask what things mean. It isn't your area of expertise and nobody would expect you to know these things. For your convenience, I have put together a list of some commonly used terms that might come in handy now and over the course of working with a lawyer.

The Action	The legal action, the matter.
Affidavit	A written statement, sworn on oath to be true.
Barrister	Usually engaged (hired) by the solicitor. A barrister is a specialist advocate (they do the talking). The person you see in court wearing robes and a wig.
Claimant	That's you, the person making the claim.
Case	Your case, the matter, the legal action.
Defendant	The person or company you are claiming against, the other side.

Engage	To engage a firm or a lawyer – is to "hire" them to act for you.
File/Filing	To file proceedings (see proceedings).
To give instructions	The lawyer will give you advice, but they act on your instructions, that is you telling them what you want to do.
Insurer	The insurance company that insures the person/company you are claiming against.
IME	Independent Medical Examination – your lawyer may send you for an IME to obtain an opinion on your injuries. The insurer may do the same.
Lawyer	An umbrella term for solicitors and barristers.
Liability	Fault.
Litigation	A legal action.
No Win - No Fee	A widely used term to describe the way in which you have hired your lawyer. Your lawyer won't get paid unless you win the case. The opposite of this is where you pay the lawyer for the work they do, regardless of the outcome.
The Matter	Your case, the legal action.

Paralegal	A paralegal might work on your case and be supervised by a lawyer. A paralegal isn't qualified or admitted as a solicitor, but with supervision can handle the procedural day to day aspects of your case.
Party, Parties	Sorry, there is no actual party. The party or parties refers to each side of the legal case, for example: you are a party and so is the person you are claiming against.
Plaintiff	That's you, the person who is making the claim.
Proceedings	The case, now in the court process. Your lawyer will file proceedings. That means that the lawyer is filing court documents to start the court process.
Settlement	When both parties (you and the insurance company) agree to terms that finalise the claim to avoid going to a trial and letting a Judge decide the outcome. Usually the settlement will involve you receiving a sum of money to forego your right to go to trial.

Solicitor	A lawyer. You will most likely engage (hire) a solicitor to act for you.
Statutory Declaration / Stat Dec	A statutory declaration is a statement, believed to be true and sworn by the declarant (person giving the statement).
Statement	A document setting out what you believe to be true.

"I used to care about what people thought about me until one day, I tried to pay my bills with their opinions."

Unknown

1
But I'm not one of those people

It's not uncommon to worry about what people will think if you make a claim for compensation but then you also have the worry about how you will get medical assistance, pay for treatment and replace lost income. These are all valid concerns and not uncommon emotions to experience. So, is there a stigma with making a claim, and who are the people who make claims each year?

The stigma of making a claim

Whether we like it or not, there can be a stigma when it comes to making a claim for compensation.

The media have done a great job at highlighting the few undeserving "compo bludgers" who lie and attempt to cheat the system by claiming for accidents that didn't happen, or grossly exaggerating the impact of the injury. Don't get me wrong! Anyone who is fraudulent in their claim is undeserving and, like in every industry, there is always one. But we need to be careful that deserving people aren't punished for the wrongs of a few individuals.

What isn't highlighted in the media are the thousands of deserving claimants, the ones who are minding their own business, working hard to support themselves and their families and the ones who are injured through no fault of their own and whose lives are forever impacted.

They are the deserving people so why should there be a stigma with that? It's the negligent party that should be ashamed, not you!

In my experience, people who felt hesitant to pursue a claim had fears and beliefs around:

- What their peers and family might think of them.
- What their colleagues at work might think.
- Whether they would be looked over for future employment opportunities because they had made a claim.
- That it was just bad luck and their lot in life to deal with it alone.

Thousands of deserving claimants are awarded compensation every year in Australia.

Are these claimants all bludgers and undeserving? Absolutely not! Every award of compensation is calculated by reference to the person's injury, the impact on the person's ability to work in the past and future, to necessary medical treatment in the past and future and care and assistance that might be necessary.

It certainly isn't a windfall, nor is it an amount of money calculated to punish the negligent party. It is simply an amount of money to put the injured person in the position they would have been if the accident hadn't happened. As we go on, I'll talk more about this.

I met with many new clients in my career and this idea of not wanting to be seen as a compo bludger was one that came up a lot. Prospective clients would say things like: "I don't know if I'm that type of person"; "What about what my workmates and boss will think?"; "This isn't the type of thing I'd normally do".

If you are making a claim for yourself, I think there is only one thing that matters, that is: "What is the best for you and your family, now and in the years to come"? What other people think is irrelevant and none of your business. If they want to judge you for doing what is best for you and your family, their judgement says more about them than it does about you.

So, what is the best for you and your family? To help you to answer this question it might be helpful to give consideration to:

- What is the nature of the injury?
- Are you at risk of ongoing issues because of the injury (physical or psychological)?
- Have you lost income as a result of the injury?
- Are you going to lose income in the future because of the injury?
- Have you incurred medical expenses?
- Will you incur treatment costs in the future?
- Do you need assistance around the home or caring for yourself as a result of the injury?

Some of these questions you may not be able to fully answer right now. Sometimes, the long-term impact of an injury can't be known right now as it can, in some cases, take years for an injury to stabilise. By stabilise, I mean that you have had the available and recommended treatment, surgery etc and have reached a point where you aren't getting better and aren't getting worse. It is just what it is. Even though you might not have exact and precise answers to these questions right now, they are still worth considering.

If you have had a meeting with a lawyer already, it is likely they have asked very similar questions to help them establish if your claim is one that is worth pursuing.

No Win – No Fee

In the field of personal injury law, most lawyers will offer you a "No Win - No Fee" arrangement. I will discuss what this all means in more detail later. But the bottom line is that if you don't win your case, the lawyer doesn't get paid. So, if the lawyer is telling you that they are prepared to take your case on, they obviously think it's a case worth running.

Law firms are costly to operate and the lawyers can work on a case for years before they get paid and they would go out of business pretty quickly if they ran claims without merit. Also, lawyers don't want to take on cases for the rogues, they risk not getting paid and it potentially damages their reputation too. So, if the lawyer is offering to act for you, not only do they think the claim has merit but they think you are a deserving claimant as well.

So, you've considered what is best for your family, you have a lawyer prepared to take the case on and maybe you are still worried about what people will think. The people who matter know you and know your true character.

The people who will judge, will judge you anyway, regardless of what you do and won't be there to fund your medical bills in the years to come or cover your lost wages. Bringing a claim isn't a short-term fix. It is about securing your future for the many years ahead.

It is very common to worry about the stigma of making a claim and to worry about what other people think. The decision to make a claim or not, should not be based on maintaining a desirable image to others.

Careful consideration should be given to the circumstances of the accident, the injury, your need for treatment, your ability to perform your work now and in the future. These are very important considerations for your future and the future of your family.

Essential points from chapter 1

- It is common to worry about the stigma of being someone who has made a claim.
- If you know you are being honest, other people's opinions really shouldn't matter.
- Making a claim is not a short-term fix. The claim is about putting you back, as best as can be done in the position you would have been in, if the accident hadn't happened. This is important for your future and the future of your family.

Chapter One - Key Questions to Consider

Working through your emotions and thoughts is sometimes helpful, just to get thoughts out on paper can help. I know sometimes when something is bothering me and when I see it there in writing, I realise how trivial it really is and other times it helps get my thoughts out in one place which makes it easier to process.

1. How are you feeling about contacting a lawyer to enquire if they can assist you in a claim for compensation?

2. Do you have thoughts about what people will think if you make a claim for compensation? If so, who's opinion is worrying you? Why are these opinions so important to you? Will you be placing too much value on these opinions?

3. Have you considered what is best for you and your family's future? (you may not fully know these answers depending on how recent the injury was incurred).

   a. What is the nature of the injury?

   b. Are you at risk of ongoing issues because of the injury (physical or psychological)?

   c. Have you lost income as a result of the injury?

d. Are you going to lose income in the future because of the injury?

e. Have you incurred medical expenses?

f. Will you incur treatment costs in the future?

g. Do you need assistance around the home or caring for yourself as a result of the injury?

4. Do you believe it might be in your and your family's best interests to at least contact a lawyer to enquire whether you might have a viable claim?

"Rapport equals trust plus comfort"

Neil Strauss

2

How to pick a lawyer

Where do you even start with finding a lawyer who is right for you and your circumstances? Let's explore some factors to consider in selecting the lawyer that is right for you like: their speciality, location and how they make you feel.

A specialist?

I see and hear personal injury advertising everywhere: billboards, internet, radio and on the television. I often wonder if I notice them because I worked in the industry for so long or whether everyone notices them. Regardless, you aren't going to have to look too hard to find the name of a personal injury lawyer.

Did you notice that I said, "personal injury lawyer"? I am a firm believer that you need a lawyer who concentrates only on personal injuries to act for you. The laws are highly technical and ever changing and you have to be sure that your lawyer is across that so they can do the best job for you. Perhaps you have a family lawyer who has always taken care of your affairs, who you trust in a great deal. In that case, I would be inclined to ask that lawyer for a referral to a lawyer whose focus is in the injury space. Much like you would ask your trusted GP for a referral to a specialist doctor if you had a specific medical concern.

Location

I was often asked if living close to the firm was important. I have acted for people who lived far and close and regardless they were able to achieve great results. What is more important than living close is the ability to be in touch and to communicate. With modern technology and even the postal service, where you live becomes less important.

If you live in a regional area, you may need to travel to the city at a few important stages of the claim, not because of where your lawyer is, but for access to medical specialists for opinion and to negotiate with the insurer. Where the lawyer is located wouldn't be a deal breaker for me in deciding who to pick to represent me.

Many lawyers will offer a home visit or an online meeting to meet with you. They understand in this field they are dealing with injured people, and they want to make this as easy as they can for you. If the lawyer offers to come to your home, it isn't some creepy way to get into your home. They really are just trying to do what is easiest for you and to meet you in a place where you will be comfortable.

A straight shooter

A claim can take upwards of 18 months from injury to settle. So, you will be working with this lawyer for a long time. My recommendation is that you should look for someone who you can talk to, and makes you feel comfortable to ask important questions.

As a lawyer, I think that not all conversations with clients are easy. Sometimes, the lawyer hasn't got good news and things don't go your way. Your lawyer might get a witness statement or medical report that doesn't support your case. This is the reason why we have lawyers, to sort through the evidence and advise you accordingly.

You want someone who will be upfront and tell you exactly what the lay of the land is, no matter what. I have seen lawyers avoid these conversations and cases have run way too long, causing unnecessary costs and emotional angst for the client when they could have been dealt with much earlier if someone was prepared to have the upfront and direct conversation with the client.

So how do you know if a lawyer will be prepared to have the hard discussions and be upfront with you? There is one big red flag to look out for. In most initial consultations the client asks: "So, roughly what do you think the case is worth, just a ballpark figure will do?" I completely understand why the question is asked. Of course, you are trying to work out if it's worth your while, and what your future might hold. Here's the thing, no one can answer that question without a crystal ball.

When a claim settles, it is a "once and for all" payment. You don't get to come back for more money later if things get worse. Equally, you don't give the money back if things go better than predicted either. So, before any lawyer can advise you on the likely value of a claim, they need to understand the long term impact of your injury. Nobody can understand that until you have had the recommended treatment, given your body time to recover and have an understanding of the impact of the injury on your employment.

After explaining this, I'd still have a few prospective clients saying: "Yeah, but come on, you must have an idea of how much will it be. I met another lawyer last week and he told me it would definitely be worth over $200,000". The answer to that is still: "No, I can't give you a dollar figure yet." As tempting as it would be to say: "Sure, you'll get about $500,000" to keep you happy and hopefully encourage you to pick me for the job, it just isn't possible to say.

I have met with prospective clients who in that moment, shortly after the accident, look to have catastrophic injuries but go on to make an amazing recovery.

I remember meeting with the family of a loved one who had been crushed on a worksite and was in hospital in an induced coma. On the face of it, you might think, that claim is going to be massive. Here's the thing though, I have never seen a more remarkable recovery in my career. That client went on to make a fantastic recovery both physically and emotionally and while he couldn't return to his original job he retrained as a truck driver.

He was compensated for the fact that he had an injury, and he was earning less than he did in his initial career. But, if I had played the "guess what my claim is worth" game, I would have set that client and his family up with completely false expectations and it would be just that, a guess.

On the flip side, I have had prospective clients with what appears to be simple injuries and you would expect they will make a good recovery, albeit they will suffer some loss as a result of the injury. On the face of it, if you were to guess, you may think it would be a modest claim at best. Some of these people have gone on, to have the most unexpected complications which have resulted in catastrophic losses for them. Again, if I played the guessing game at the outset with a prospective client like this, they may have just decided the claim wasn't worth pursuing.

So, as you can see, without time, treatment and medical evidence, there is no way that anyone can tell you what your claim is worth. A good lawyer will explain this and will work to gather the best evidence to support your claim.

There were many times when I would have loved to say to a prospect that it'll be okay and you will definitely win the case and I can get you the money to pay that mortgage off, knowing it would give them peace of mind and they would most certainly pick me as their lawyer.

But really, what if the evidence didn't stack up? What if they made a great recovery and relied on that advice believing a big pay day was coming? In that case, as a lawyer, I haven't acted in the interests of the client at all and that is your lawyer's paramount duty, to act in your best interests.

If a lawyer is telling you what you want to hear in that first appointment and they are already avoiding explaining why they can't tell you what you want to hear, what are they going to be like during the claim if things get tough? Pick someone who you know is a straight shooter and can have the difficult conversation if needed.

What's the vibe? Trust and Rapport

You will most likely first talk to your potential lawyer on the phone and hopefully soon meet the person or talk face to face online. In those initial few interactions, the lawyer will be attempting to gather the facts to assess whether you have a case worth pursuing. Your goal in this time should be to see if you have good rapport with the lawyer. So:

- Do you feel like you can comfortably ask questions?
- Are you feeling heard?
- Do you feel like they care and have your best interests as their focus?

It can be hard to put into words what is necessary for a person to establish trust and rapport because it's a feeling for the individual person. For those of who you have watched the classic Australian film "The Castle", you know, it's "The Vibe".

Google

It's the way of the online world now, isn't it? We Google directions, recommendations and the answers to just about anything are there on the internet. Well, maybe as a final check, you should do a quick google check of the law firm and the lawyer's name, just to be sure that they aren't embroiled in controversy. If they are busy fighting tax debts and bankruptcy, chances are that they will be distracted and won't have the time to focus on you and your matter.

Will I need to pay to just meet and get some initial advice?

In my experience almost all lawyers will offer a "No Win - No Fee" agreement and to be in a position to offer that, they need to know a few facts first. Sometimes once they get the facts, they decide that it isn't a case they would take on and there is no fee issued to the prospective client. The best thing to do here is to ask, and things will be clear for everyone. Some suggested questions to ask before an initial appointment are:

1. If we meet and you decide that it isn't a case you'd take on, will you issue me with a bill for your time or expenses incurred?

2. If we meet and you decide it is a case you will take on, but I don't want to engage your firm, will you issue me with a bill for your time and expenses incurred?

I would be very surprised if any lawyer answered "Yes" to these questions because it is a competitive market for the lawyers, and they will want to act for you if your case has merit.

In choosing the lawyer that is right for you and your case I recommend focussing on: their speciality, how you will communicate with them, how at ease you are with them to ask questions and whether you trust the lawyer to be upfront with you.

Essential points from chapter 2

- Injury law is a complex area of law with a lot of processes with important time frames. For that reason, I would recommend working with a lawyer who focusses on injury law.
- The physical location of the lawyer would not be a key factor in deciding who to work with for me.
- Is your lawyer telling you what you want to hear to keep things easy and increase your chances of hiring them? You want someone who is a straight shooter and will have a difficult conversation with you.
- You need to work with the lawyer for a significant amount of time and it is a matter that is incredibly important to you. Work with someone you have a good rapport with.
- In the personal injury field, most lawyers will offer you a free first consultation to meet you and establish if it is something they can help with.

Chapter 2: Check List

If you have met with a lawyer and still aren't sure if it is the right lawyer for you, here is a list of considerations to help you to make a decision.

		YES	NO
1.	Does the lawyer mostly focus on personal injury claims?		
2.	Is it clear how you will communicate with the lawyer, eg. Email, Zoom, in person, by letter etc.		
3.	Does the lawyer expect you to travel to their office? If so, is that viable for you?		
4.	Did the lawyer make you feel at ease?		
5.	Did the lawyer make you feel like it was okay to ask questions?		
6.	Did you feel heard?		
7.	When you asked questions, did the lawyer answer them clearly and directly?		

8.	Do you feel like the lawyer explained things well to you?		
9.	Was there anything you heard that you didn't like to hear, but the lawyer took the time to explain why it was that way?		
10.	Has anyone made recommendations about the lawyer, either directly or online?		

"A verbal contract isn't worth the paper it's written on."

Samuel Goldwyn

3

Signing a costs agreement

Costs agreements, contracts, client agreements, disclosure statements and the list goes on, it can be overwhelming! Here we will discuss what the lawyer will want you to sign and why.

No Win - No Fee

When someone suffers an injury, it often impacts on their ability to work and earn income and can add financial strain to the household. Not many injured people are in a position to pay legal fees upfront. Many deserving people would not have the ability to seek compensation if it wasn't for a "No Win - No Fee" agreement.

"No Win - No Fee" means that the law firm does not issue you with a bill for fees unless you are successful in your case and are awarded compensation. Then you pay the legal fees from your compensation.

Once the lawyer has enough information to decide if your case is one which they are prepared to take on, they will want you to sign a costs agreement.

What is a costs agreement?

The costs agreement is a legal contract between you and the law firm. It will set out the terms about how your legal fees will be calculated, when they will be paid and all your responsibilities during the course of the claim.

When a lawyer asks you to sign a legal contract with them, it is understandable that you might be a bit nervous entering into a contract with a lawyer. It is important for you to not sign anything that you don't understand and make sure to ask questions if you are unsure of anything.

Why is the costs agreement necessary?

The lawyers aren't just creating work and extra paper by asking you to sign a costs agreement. There are legal requirements that they do this, so it isn't a case that only some lawyers want you to sign an agreement and others won't require one.

Each of the states and territories have their own rules about costs agreements and what is required. My view is that the main reason the agreements exist is for consumer protection. It means that people making a claim know the terms upfront and the lawyer is limited to charging fees in accordance with the agreement and they can't just charge more because you got a larger settlement. When it comes to legal fees, no one wants surprises. Having the costs agreement means that there should be no surprises and both, you and the law firm should understand your rights and responsibilities.

Before you sign a costs agreement

A good lawyer should talk you through the agreement and explain in their own words and in simple language what each part means for you.

If you have questions about the agreement, you must ask, no question is too silly. If you aren't comfortable enough to ask the lawyer a question about the agreement, or they are dismissive of your question, how are you going to work together on your case? This can be a long process and you don't want those niggling unanswered questions to hang over you.

You always have the right to seek independent advice before signing the agreement and you can check your local "Law Society" or "Legal Services Commission" for any publications on what to look for in a costs agreement. I have listed those links below for you.

Like anything in life, don't sign anything that you aren't comfortable with or understand.

State and territory resources

Queensland Legal Services Commission	https://www.lsc.qld.gov.au/
Queensland Law Society	https://www.qls.com.au/Home
NSW Office of the Legal Services Commission	http://www.olsc.nsw.gov.au/
NSW Law Society	https://www.lawsociety.com.au/
ACT	https://www.actlawsociety.asn.au/
Law Institute Victoria	https://www.liv.asn.au/
Victorian Legal Services Board and Commissioner	https://lsbc.vic.gov.au/consumers/choosing-and-working-your-lawyer
Law Society of Tasmania	https://lst.org.au/public-info/legal-costs/
Legal Services Board of Tasmania	https://www.lpbt.com.au/
Legal Services Commission of South Australia	https://lsc.sa.gov.au/

Signing a costs agreement

Law Society of SA	https://www.lawsocietysa.asn.au/Public/Publications/Resources_Search/Community%20Resources.aspx
Law Society of WA	https://www.lawsocietywa.asn.au/
Legal Practice Board of WA	https://www.lpbwa.org.au/Home.aspx
WA	https://www.lawsocietywa.asn.au/how-much-will-it-cost/
Law Society NT	https://lawsocietynt.asn.au/for-the-community/legal-costs-information-1.html

Essential points from chapter 3

- It is normal and a necessary requirement for the law firm to enter into a costs agreement with you.
- DO NOT sign anything that you do not understand!
- Ask questions until you are satisfied and understand everything before you sign anything.

"If you think it's expensive to hire a professional to do the job, wait until you hire an amateur."

Red Adair

4

Keeping costs down

How much is this going to cost? It was usually one of the first things I would be asked as a lawyer. It's a common concern and the good news is that there are things that you can do to assist your lawyer and keep the costs down.

So, you have engaged a lawyer. Time is money so to speak. There is work to be done to protect your interests, gather evidence and get you a result. You don't want the lawyer to spend a short time on the case because you will achieve nothing, albeit their costs will be minimal.

As a child, I remember hearing how lawyers have a big stopwatch on their desk and they charge for every minute of their time. By the way, this is not what attracted me to a career in law. As crazy as this image is, it's kind of true.

The first step is to understand how you are being charged. It is set out in the costs agreement that you would have signed. Have a look over the agreement and get an understanding of how you are being charged.

Does your agreement allow for a task-based fee, a time-based fee or perhaps a fixed fee? Most common is a time-based agreement. If it isn't clear to you from the costs agreement, ask the lawyer how their fees are calculated. This is not an unreasonable question.

There may be different people in a legal team working on your claim, for example: the lawyer will do the more technical work and a paralegal might draft some documents and the secretary will take care of the more administrative calls and letters.

Knowing who the people in your legal team are and what they do, as well as how you will be charged for their time is helpful. For example, the secretary's time may cost a fraction of the lawyer's time. If you had to let them know that you were able to attend a medical appointment they have made for you, you really don't need to personally speak to a lawyer with this information, this is something that the secretary could make a note of. By speaking to the secretary to confirm something administrative that is not a technical or legal issue, you will have most likely saved yourself some money.

A good lawyer will spend their time working on the procedural, red tape matters and making sure that your claim is protected, gathering evidence to support your claim and preparing for trial.

Very few matters go to trial and most of them settle before trial. You can ask your lawyer for the current statistics around this. What you want your lawyer working on, and to be paying them for, is their time in progressing your claim. There is an amount of work that needs to be done on every claim no matter how big or small the claim is. So, what can you do to keep the costs down?

Respond promptly to the lawyers' requests for information

Firstly, respond to the lawyers' request for information as soon as possible. This not only will assist incurring unnecessary costs, but you will also keep your claim moving forward and avoid unnecessary delays. You are paying for every time that the law firm calls, emails or writes to you. You don't want to be incurring costs for letters asking you to hurry up and respond. You want the lawyer using their time to do the technical work you engaged them to do, not calling you to chase you up.

Pass on necessary information to the case

If your employment or medical circumstances change, then your lawyer needs to know. It is important that you pass that information on at the earliest convenience. Your lawyer should tell you the types of things they need to be told.

For example: if you took a new job, it is important that your lawyer knows who you work for, what your position is, what tasks you will be performing and how much you are being paid. If you fail to update the lawyer, the lawyer may be preparing documents with old information and it could result in doubling up on work and they will need to update it all at a later time.

The same goes for medical treatment and information. It is important for your lawyer to be up to date so they will be working with the most up to date relevant facts.

Emotion

It is understandable and there is no doubt that you may be feeling anxious as well as angry. Anxious for what the future holds, and angry at what has happened to you. These are completely understandable emotions given what has happened.

Sometimes, it can help to talk through our emotions, and it is helpful to have someone to talk to, maybe a doctor, counsellor, friends or family. When you are speaking with your lawyer, I recommend you ask yourself: "Are you telling your lawyer essential information for your case, or are you venting?"

If you are venting, and you choose to vent to your lawyer, it's important to realise it isn't new information that will advance your case and could be costing you $120 for a ten-minute vent. You might feel better in that moment, but you aren't going to feel better when you see the bill! The reality is that it'd be cheaper to buy a friend a coffee and have them hear you out when you just need to get something off your chest.

In my experience, this is the area where the greatest amount of costs are incurred and could have been avoided. As lawyers, yes, we are human and have a heart, but we aren't helping you if we sit on the phone crying with you all day. Lawyers want to get on with the job and bring your case to the best conclusion for you. That is what you are paying them for.

You don't want the case unnecessarily dragged out either, so costs aside, what do you want your lawyer spending their time on: being your most expensive friend and listening to you vent, or working on and progressing your claim?

6-minute time blocks

Remember that movie "The Firm", with Tom Cruise? It was all about charging in 6-minute blocks, even when a task takes 1 minute, the lawyers were charging for 6 minutes. This is a very common way of billing in law practices. There are 10 lots of 6 minutes in every hour and lawyers charge each 6-minute block to a client for work done.

So, let's say you call your lawyer and speak for 2 minutes, you will be charged for 6 minutes.

- Speak for 5 minutes you get charged for 6 minutes.
- Speak for 6 minutes and you get charged for 6 minutes.
- Speak for 7 minutes and you get charged for 12 minutes (2 lots of 6)
- Speak for 8 minutes and you get charged for 12 minutes and so on....

So, have a look at your costs agreement and understand how time is charged when the legal team work on your case.

In my opinion, you might as well maximise that time. If you are getting charged for 6 minutes, you might as well use it up! And if you are on a call and your question is answered at the 5-minute mark, get off the call before you tick over the 6 minute mark and get charged for another 6 minute unit of time. This also allows your lawyer to get on with progressing your case and to work efficiently.

Make a list

Make a list of your questions or information you need to tell the lawyer. That way you don't get distracted, and you will make the best use of the time. You also avoid forgetting something and having to call a second or third time for the same question.

A list of questions is handy too. If they aren't urgent matters, you can keep adding to the list until you have a few matters to discuss and then that way you make the best use of everyone's time.

Take notes

It can be a good idea to take notes of what your lawyer is telling you.

Understandably, clients are often anxious about what their future holds and that can make it difficult to take in everything the lawyer is telling you. Also, there can be a lot of new information to take in at once and often it isn't until later when you go home and process it that you start to think: "Hang on, did they say x or y?".

My recommendation is to take a few notes and that way you can always read over them and save yourself another call to the lawyer to clarify what they said.

Record Keeping

In any case you need evidence, so your lawyer will be asking for documentation to prove certain aspects of your case. That could be: income tax records, medical receipts, home help receipts etc. The better organised this information is, means your lawyer can get their job done without spending time sorting through your records.

Having documents sorted in some kind of easy-to-understand order means that you aren't paying for a lawyer's time to sort through documents. It means they can get on with their job in preparing your claim.

An example of well sorted documents might be an "excel spreadsheet" summarising medical expenses, or a neat bundle of receipts in date order with details of what they are for. Not so great, is the shoebox filled with receipts for all household expenses that year, some accident related, some not and the lawyer is left to make sense of it all.

Don't laugh, it happens! And, whether your lawyer will admit it or not, it is human nature that we are drawn to the simple tasks first. So, as a lawyer I can tell you that I'd be more inclined to put that well organised file to the top of the pile of work for the day and I'd be hoping that shoebox of receipts would sort itself out and disappear. That is the sort of work that tends to get put off.

The lesson here, make it as simple as you can for your legal team. It will save unnecessarily rising costs and your work is more likely to get done without delay.

Don't keep asking the same question hoping for a different answer!

I used to get this one a lot! I get it. It's an uncertain time when you have all sorts of fears, and you want to be reassured. But you can ask the lawyer over and over what your claim is worth, whether you should take a job that the doctor says you can do, when the claim will settle or whatever it is that you are wanting to know. Sometimes you either aren't going to like the answer, or the answer is that the lawyer can't give you a definite answer until X, Y, Z happens.

You can keep asking, but the answers won't change and the only thing that changes is your legal fees, they go up.

Ask

While the processes are similar for each claim, the circumstances are unique. I think it is a reasonable question to put to your lawyer: "What can I do to help keep costs down and keep the matter progressing"?

If you engage a lawyer, it is only fair that they will be paid for the work they did to secure you a result. However, by keeping these tips in mind, you can make the lawyer's job easier, keep your claim progressing in a timely manner and save your own costs unnecessarily inflating.

Essential points from chapter 4

- Respond promptly to requests that are made by your lawyer.
- Pass on important information to your lawyer.
- Try to keep it to the facts and put emotion to the side.
- Think about time! If your lawyer is charging on a time basis, maybe you don't have a 10-minute conversation about the weekend.
- Keep a list of things to talk to your lawyer about, to keep you on track.
- Take notes of what your lawyer is telling you, to save asking the same questions over and over.
- When sending information to your lawyer, make it as simple as possible.
- Ask your lawyer what you can do to keep costs down.

"You got to know when to hold them, know when to fold them, know when to walk away, know when to run."

Kenny Rogers

5

Can I change lawyers?

When you are feeling like you aren't making progress, being heard, or perhaps hearing what you want to hear, a thought may cross your mind that maybe you don't have the best lawyer acting for you. Is it possible to change lawyers midway through a claim? Is it necessary? Is it worth it? Or are you better with the devil that you know, so to speak?

It's your claim

The quick answer is: Yes, you can withdraw instructions from the lawyer acting for you and instruct another lawyer to represent you. Of course, it is never that simple because there are a few things to consider first.

Why would you want to change lawyers?

While I hope that you have engaged a lawyer who is doing a great job and you are feeling comfortable with the process, this isn't always the case. The four main reasons that most commonly spark discontent and raise questions about looking for a new lawyer are:

- The lawyer isn't keeping you up to date and you feel like you always have to ask to be told what is happening and what stage things are at;
- The claim is taking too long;
- The lawyer never takes or returns your calls; or
- You don't like the advice of your lawyer.

If this is how you are feeling, before you start searching for a new lawyer, I would encourage you to really, as objectively as you can, look at exactly what is going on versus how you are feeling.

I have prepared some questions at the end of this chapter for you to work through to help you to examine whether you are just nervous or frustrated at the process or possible outcome, or whether it is actually a case where the lawyer is not doing the best job for you. The reason for this is that if it is just the process you are frustrated at, changing lawyers isn't going to change anything and you will find yourself in a situation where the only thing that changed was the name of your lawyer.

Is there another option?

Assuming you have looked at the situation and you really believe there is an issue, is there an alternative to finding a new lawyer? Could there be a simpler solution?

Are your concerns something you can discuss with the lawyer? In my experience, these conversations are always better once the emotions have settled. By asking questions and raising your concerns, there could be a simple solution, perhaps a misunderstanding, and you can both agree on a path forward.

Perhaps the circumstances of what is going on isn't something you can discuss with your lawyer. Is your lawyer part of a bigger firm? Who do they report to? Often there is a "Practice Group Leader" or a Senior Lawyer, or a General Manager of the firm that you can talk to.

Often in the agreements that you signed there will be a section on who to contact if you are not satisfied or have concerns. It could be that a quick call to that person will have the situation resolved quickly for you.

In larger firms it may be a solution that a new lawyer in that firm could take over your matter. The agreements that you have signed are between you and the firm, not the individual lawyer, so this may be a very simple solution to keep your matter moving forward and pair you with someone who you believe that will do the best job.

Delay & increasing costs

Something to consider is that if you engage a new lawyer, it might cause delay in your matter. The new lawyer will have to get up to speed with your case. How much material is there for the lawyer to get across? Of course, this will vary from case to case. There is a risk of the legal costs increasing as the new lawyer has to get across and revise material and the steps already taken.

These concerns have to be balanced with the best job being done for you too. It may be any delay and increase in costs, is so minor compared to the risk of continuing with the current lawyer.

Will the first lawyer agree to defer their fees?

It is common practice for the lawyer releasing the file to the new lawyer to agree to be paid at the successful conclusion of your claim. What does your costs agreement say? Hopefully you kept a copy of the agreement, and you can show that to your prospective new lawyer who can advise you and take care of any negotiations as to what, how and when they get paid.

To save the risk of delay and increasing costs, in my opinion you would try to do everything possible to make it work with your lawyer before you withdrew instructions and told them not to act for you anymore. You should have an open and frank discussion with the lawyer, or their supervisor about your concerns and be certain that your concerns can't be put to rest before you go looking for a new lawyer.

Essential points from chapter 5

- Examine what it is that is causing you to ask if you have the right lawyer for your case. Will changing lawyers really change anything?
- As a client, you give instructions to act and it is your choice to give or withdraw those instructions to act. It is your decision and choice whether a lawyer continues to act for you.
- Would there be any significant delay or increase in costs by changing lawyers?
- Have you explored other solutions like discussing the issue with the lawyer or someone more senior in the firm?

Chapter 5 – Questions

To help you work through your concerns, I have listed the four main areas that cause people concerns and some further questions to consider.

My lawyer isn't keeping me updated. I feel like I am always chasing them to find out what is going on.

What you want to establish is: Does it just feel like not much is happening, or do you really not know what is happening? There can be large periods of time where not much happens in a claim, but this is expected and you don't need your lawyer writing to you weekly to say "not much has happened this week, as expected."

- When did you last get an email or letter from your lawyer?
- Does that correspondence help with understanding what will happen and what to expect next?
- Has the lawyer explained that nothing will happen for several months? If so, maybe they have nothing to update you on and that is why you haven't heard from them in a long time.
- Could you ask the lawyer what the future steps are and for an associated timeline?

The claim is taking too long. What do I do?

You need an understanding of whether the claim is taking too long in your view, or whether it is taking too long compared to what the lawyer told you to expect. If it is within what your lawyer advised you would happen, engaging a new lawyer isn't going to change anything.

- What advice did the lawyer give you about length of time of the claim?
- Are you within that timeframe of what the lawyer told you?
- If the claim is taking longer than the initial advice given, has the lawyer explained to you why this has happened?
- Is the lawyer able to give you advice on some sort of timeline for the claim? If not, can they explain why or what it will depend on?

The lawyer never takes or returns my calls.

Do you have an expectation that your lawyer should be at their desk, available to take your call every time you ring? Or is there an actual issue with the lawyer's conduct?

- When you leave a message, how long does it take for a return call? Did the agreement, their website or any customer service promises set out terms for returning calls within certain time frames?

- If you escalate this to a more senior lawyer in the firm, what are their expectations with regards to a reasonable time frame for calls to be returned?
- Did the assistant give you a time frame that the call would be returned in? Or could you ask that question?
- Did someone else in the team call you back and assist you to save the costs of the lawyer being involved?

I don't like what my lawyer is telling me.

You need to understand if you just don't like the advice, or whether the advice is based on the wrong facts and is flawed in some way. Putting the same evidence and facts with a new lawyer, probably isn't going to change what the lawyers are telling you.

- Is there some medical, financial or other evidence missing that would change the opinion of the lawyer?
- Are the facts the lawyer is basing their opinion on, correct?
- Has something medical, financial etc been overlooked and not considered?
- Does it just seem really unfair? Is it the law and rules that you don't like?

"Be patient. Some things take time."

Unknown

6

Why is the claim taking so long?

What's the saying? Time flies when you are having fun! I don't think I have ever had a client comment on how quickly a claim was running. It's fair to say that dealing with lawyers and the legal process probably isn't most people's idea of fun.

The length of time to reach a conclusion on a claim can be very stressful for people. Understanding why there is no quick fix and what a realistic time frame is, and some mindset techniques can help you work through any frustrations that you have with this.

How long is a long time?

Time is relative, what might seem a long time to one person isn't long to another.

If your lawyer has set some realistic time frames for you, I recommend using that as a reference for time.

For example: If the lawyer was saying that they expect that the claim should take 18 months, anything within that time frame isn't anything to worry about.

A constant worry about how long it will take can consume and drain you and the worry won't change the time frame or outcomes. If you are able to accept the lawyer's advice on this, even if you don't like the advice, it will free you to put your energy to far more productive things.

While having acted for many injured people, I think one of the most difficult things that they face is being asked to look backwards when they want to look forwards.

The lawyers, doctors and insurers want to know, what happened, how did it happen, how did it feel, what couldn't you do, what can't you do now? This can feel like you are constantly reliving the event and the injury. I think this also adds to the feeling like the claim is taking a long time.

Having an awareness that you are going to be asked to look back and recount events is important. As much as you can compartmentalise that you need to do that for the lawyers, but otherwise you are looking forwards will be so helpful to you, your mindset and recovery. Being able to take your thoughts back for the lawyers, but otherwise having a mindset in the present and looking to what you want is going to assist you in your recovery and I think the time taken on the claim won't feel as long either.

Some of our stories in chapter 9 share their experiences with this issue and how they managed this and what they might do differently if the situation arose again.

It isn't a quick fix

Sadly, your case isn't going to be resolved as quickly as an episode of "Law and Order" and dealing with lawyers won't be as exciting as watching "Ally McBeal".

I remember working with a client and we reached a point where we were meeting with the insurer and their lawyers to negotiate a settlement. She looked at me and said "Is this it? Is this what you do all day?". I didn't quite pick up on what she meant at first, so she elaborated for me in very straightforward terms: "This is so boring, it's not like television at all!". -No, no it isn't!

I don't know you and your specific circumstances, and this book is not designed to give legal advice, so I won't be stating time frames here. If you have a lawyer acting for you and you are reading this chapter and wondering why the claim is taking so long, you need to have a discussion with your lawyer.

There are many valid reasons why your claim can't be settled quickly after an accident, but a good lawyer should explain those reasons to you. Sometimes it isn't what you want to hear but understanding why and why it is necessary to take those steps to best look after your interests is important.

Before you can settle

Common things that have to happen before a claim can be settled are:

- Forms, claim documents, certificates to be given to the insurer;
- Time frames for the insurer to respond (all set out in legislation);
- Treatment (physiotherapy, surgery etc) to be completed;
- Your injury has reached a point where it is stable (not getting better and not getting worse).

Hopefully these are some of the things that your lawyer has discussed with you.

But I haven't heard from the lawyer in so long

But it has been months since you have heard anything, and you are starting to worry?

Have a look over the letters from your lawyer. A good lawyer will have set out the time frames and next steps.

For example: If you have submitted a claim form and the insurer has 6 months to respond, you might not hear much for 6 months.

In that case, hopefully your lawyer has written to you explaining that it might be quiet for 6 months and has let you know what they expect you to do over that time. For example: Keep tracking any time off work and expenses incurred. If that is the case, and you haven't heard much, I don't think there is anything to worry about.

However, if you look over the letters and emails from your lawyer and no time frames are set out and you genuinely have no idea what is happening next, then I would be giving the lawyer a call and asking them what the next steps are and how long those steps should take.

Lawyers – educated, respected, arguably devoid of emotions, living a fast and glamorous life – are human too. Lawyers can get overwhelmed or overworked. How do you know when it is just a time in the case when not much is happening versus the lawyer not coping or not doing a great job?

A good lawyer should have communicated clearly to you, what the next steps are and what to expect each step of the way. Sometimes it isn't what we want to hear, but if you take an honest look at the letters, it is there and have they have explained what to expect.

A red flag is where there is no explanation about what to expect next. If that is the case and your calls aren't being returned in a few days, it is worth reaching up in the law firm to see what is going on. Sometimes in the costs agreement, the firm has set out who to contact if you are not happy, otherwise, a quick search of their website should make it clear who to contact.

It is worth making a call and just raising your concerns that it isn't clear to you what the next steps are, the associated time frames and that your calls aren't being returned? Communication is key here, so you should have the conversation rather than letting the worry build in your mind.

Awareness is everything here. With an understanding of a realistic time frame and keeping your focus on that, rather than whether that seems fair or why it has to be that way, you can save yourself many hours of unnecessary frustration.

Essential points from chapter 6

- What has your lawyer advised you is a reasonable time frame? If they haven't talked about this, ask the question.
- Is the claim running on a time frame based on the lawyer's advice? If not, has the lawyer explained why time frames have changed?
- Where are your thoughts? Are you living the injury and event over and over? What can you do to make a shift in thoughts and focus?

"Everyone on the internet is an expert in everything"

Unknown

7

"But my friend said…"

Everyone has an opinion. And that is the problem. Managing well-meaning advice from family and friends can leave you feeling confused and exhausted.

Well-meaning family and friends

If I had a dollar for every time a client responded to my advice with, "But my friend said….".

So, everyone knows someone, or someone who knows someone else who has made a claim for compensation following an injury.

Your well-meaning friends, family, neighbours or even doctor may try to give you some tips on your case ranging from which lawyer to use, the process, how successful it will be or even how much the case will likely settle for and when. Of course, their tips are based on the experience of someone they know or know of, but every case has to be assessed on its own facts and the laws at the time. Without a detailed understanding of medical opinion, work history and earning history, it is impossible for anyone to give any relevant advice on your matter.

It isn't uncommon for clients to ask their lawyer about these comparisons and stories that they have been told of. Raising that they heard claims that have settled like: "How come my neighbour's son got $200,000 and he only had a broken leg?".

My answer was always the same, without a detailed understanding of the facts of that case I really can't comment on why it settled the way it did. The example case could even be from a different state where different laws apply. The fact that you can tell them it's about a 20-year-old truck driver with a leg injury, really isn't enough facts for a lawyer to give an opinion, not even a ballpark opinion on the value of the case. So, you can ask your lawyer if you want about the case your friend told you about, but save yourself the money and read this chapter over and over if you have to.

Your family and friends are well-meaning and are coming from a good place. They will no doubt want the best for you and in their own way are trying to help you. My advice is that you can say with certainty to anyone telling you about other cases and asking questions of why yours isn't the same that your lawyer is gathering all the specific vital information for your case and every case is different.

And what about your doctor that wants to give you advice on your legal matter? Would you accept medical advice from your lawyer? Let the appropriate experts take care of the matters in their field.

Google

I once heard that searching the internet to self-diagnose an illness made you a cyber-chondriact! Brilliant!

We need a similar term for people searching "Google" for legal advice. It is a long process to become legally qualified to give advice and represent people. Honestly, save yourself the time and stress and get off Google. Nothing good will come from it.

When I was pregnant, my obstetrician was quick to point out in that first appointment that my mother and grandmother and many generations before me all got through pregnancy without Google and to stay away from it. Sound advice!

You really can find whatever you want to believe online, so no clarity will come from late night trawling on the internet. If you have a genuine concern on question, give your lawyer a quick email or call to have a qualified professional answer and then you can ease your mind and put the issue to rest.

What are the risks?

If you were to repeatedly question your lawyer's advice, which by the way, unless there is a change in evidence or facts, their advice isn't going to suddenly change. You are only increasing your own legal costs to hear the same thing over and over.

Searching for what you want to hear from friends, the internet etc is going to increase the uncertainty in your own mind, in a time when you are faced with uncertainty in so many respects. This is exhausting and draining and can be all consuming if you let it. This is not good for you and for your mindset in moving forward with your life.

In an extreme case, if you were to constantly question your lawyer's opinion, hoping for a different answer, not only would you increase your own costs but you risk the matter being delayed and taking longer. Your lawyer only has so many hours a day to work. Do you want them repeating something over and over to you, or working on steps to move your case forward?

Let the experts do their work

Remember, you are paying your lawyer to act for you and give you advice. You don't need the legal opinion of your family and friends. I'm assuming they aren't legally trained and qualified. You'll need to talk about the case enough with your lawyer, which as I have already discussed can be draining, so you might as well keep conversation with family and friends to the fun stuff in life.

Just like when you get married, have a baby, buy a house, or any other big step in life, if you are making a claim, people will want to share their experience and stories with you. While they are well-meaning, they are really not helping at all. Remember, it's your lawyer that knows all the facts that make up your case, so they are the one best equipped and qualified to give you advice.

Essential points from chapter 7

- Well-meaning people will want to share stories of other claims with you and speculate on what your claim is worth, how long it will take etc. They really aren't qualified to comment on your claim.
- If you are unsure of anything, it is best to ask your lawyer, not Google.
- Your lawyer's opinion, which they are qualified to give, is based on an analysis of the specific facts of your case.
- When there is no change in facts or evidence, your lawyer's opinion is unlikely to change, no matter how many times you ask them.
- Looking outside to friends, google etc for what you want to hear can be exhausting, costly and delay your claim.

"Learn the wisdom of compromise, for it is better to bend a little than to break."

Unknown

8

Settling out of court

The decision to settle your claim or not is yours. That can be incredibly empowering and overwhelming at the same time. While it's the moment you have waited for and anticipated, it's not uncommon to have a flood of questions and fears when faced with the reality that this claim could soon be over! Understanding what your options are, what the process involves and what role your lawyer will play at this time will be the key in making the decision that is best for you.

Every claimant has a choice, to settle the claim or go to trial and let a Judge decide.

A settlement is where you and the other party come to an agreement and the terms, and any payments are agreed by both of you. The agreement is final, neither party can change their minds later. This will give you a certain outcome. You know exactly what you have agreed to and when payment is due.

If you go to trial, you are leaving the outcome to the decision of a Judge. Sometimes a reasonable settlement cannot be reached and going to trial is warranted. Each side will present their evidence before the Judge and the Judge will decide if the other party is at fault or not and how much compensation, if any, you should be awarded. Which Judge hears your case, their decision and how long they take to make a decision is out of your control.

The compensation laws are written in a way so that there are procedures in place to encourage people and create opportunity to settle out of court. This reduces legal costs and keeps the courts from overflowing with these matters.

There will come a point in your claim where you are faced with a decision to accept an offer from the insurer or to prepare to go to trial. Keep in mind, the matter may still settle before trial. It is your lawyer's job to give you advice about what they recommend you do. Ultimately, the decision is yours though, only you can make the actual decision as to what to do.

Settlement conference

A common way to settle out of court is at a settlement conference. This is a meeting where the parties like the insurer and their legal representative, you and your lawyer all meet and attempt to negotiate a settlement.

Your lawyer will explain this in greater detail if it is an appropriate step for your claim. I want to reassure if you if a settlement conference is organised, it is a completely normal step in a claim. Please don't panic wondering why this meeting is happening! It really is a meeting, "settlement conference" is just a fancy way of saying a meeting where we will try to settle your claim.

At the settlement conference, your claim might settle, and it might not, you are in control and make those decisions. Your lawyer will give you advice on what they recommend. If it doesn't settle, it's a step forward in the process and the lawyers may have been able to identify what areas it is they don't agree on, so they know where they might need to go and do more work.

It's common for people to worry about whether they will need to talk at the conference, or be asked questions etc. Quite often the insurer will want to hear from you. Until now, you are just someone that they have read about in reports. Of course, each case is different, and your lawyer should explain to you what is expected on the day and how it will be run. Again, don't be concerned if you are asked to say a few words, you haven't been singled out. This is completely normal. You won't be alone; your legal team will be by your side.

A Helping Hand

Fighting on for more money

One issue that I have witnessed is clients being advised to reject an offer of settlement and fight on because they will likely get a bigger award of compensation at trial.

When I have questioned these people on the numbers offered, what they would receive after expenses and what it is they anticipate being awarded at trial, they can only tell me: "More". They have no understanding of the numbers beyond the headline number.

What can be overlooked are the costs of fighting for more compared to how much more you are likely to be awarded by a Judge. Put simply, would you spend $20,000 to chase $1,000? How happy would you be if you were awarded $1,000 more at trial, a year and $20,000 in expenses later?

Red flag: - When your lawyer is saying: "You'll get more at trial" but not breaking down the expenses and discussing what you actually get in your pocket compared to a likely in pocket figure at trial.

I have seen this happen too many times when I had acquired files from other firms. Lawyers say to fight on and you will get more, but remember, the legal fees grow too.

I have seen this happen where clients are advised to reject an offer of settlement and push on to trial on the promise for more. But they have no understanding of how much more is likely, what the increase of fees is likely to be and most importantly what are they likely to get in their hand after all fees and deductions are made. You could push on for another year, increase costs and the lawyer gets you $1 more than was offered to you out of court. Is that a win? They delivered on their word though and you settled for more. You just won't get more in your pocket.

When you are faced with a decision regarding whether to settle or not, a good lawyer will have a very clear discussion with you around fees, refunds, risk, and what you actually get in your pocket from the settlement.

I would be very concerned if these matters were not addressed by my legal team when making a decision as to accepting an offer or proceeding to trial. Without that information, how can you make a decision about what to do?

Before you accept or reject any offer, be sure to understand exactly what the offer represents to you in your pocket or "in your hand". You can only make informed decisions once you have that information.

Every decision around offers and settlements is a very important one and one that can not be changed later. A good lawyer will explain all the risks, costs and consequences of settling. They will give you advice on what they think you should do. This is what you are paying for and it is your decision about what you want to do. If you feel like you do not have the necessary information to make a decision, it is important that you ask for the things I have discussed in this chapter.

Essential points – Chapter 8

- Every claimant has a choice to agree to a settlement or go to trial and let the Judge decide the outcome.
- Before making a decision on whether to accept or reject an offer of settlement it is important to fully understand your lawyer's advice.
- It is important to understand what any offer means to you in your pocket or in your hand after all fees, refunds and deductions are made.
- If your lawyer is not giving you advice that includes "in hand" estimates, ask the question!

"Every end is a new beginning."

Unknown

9

What happens once we settle?

It's over, and now what happens? From first being injured, the pain, loss, uncertainty, working with a lawyer, to coming to a decision to settle, or receiving a judgement, there are a lot of emotions along the way, so it's understandable that settling and having it all over will bring its own wave of emotions.

Acceptance

In all the years of acting for injured people, no one ever said to me: "I am so glad, I got injured and got to make a claim", but my goal was that people would understand why the result was whatever it was. I always thought that it was important that clients understood the advice and outcome, while they may not necessarily be happy about it. After all, most people would rather they weren't injured in the first place.

I think with a good lawyer explaining their advice and the options until the client understands why they are making the choice to settle, or not, you avoid years of the client being haunted with thoughts of whether they made the right decision or not. By understanding the advice, they can make a decision and then accept that it is done and mentally move on.

Sense of relief

I have previously discussed how some people can find that making a claim, dealing with lawyers, doctors etc can force them to re-live the event over and over and forces them to think about their injuries and what they can and can no longer do. In that case, they can experience a great sense of relief and sometimes improvement in their overall well-being when the case has come to an end. Simply not having to think about it anymore can be a wonderful thing in many respects.

In my experience, I saw many clients' overall mood and outlook improve once the claim had reached a conclusion.

Future expenses and needs

It is important for you to understand how your future needs will be covered. Future medical expenses, lost wages and care that you require is most likely at your expense, once a claim has settled. Sometimes your entitlement to social security benefits is ceased for a period after settlement.

This is something that your lawyer should discuss with you and is something you must understand before you finalise a claim.

Despite giving advice to make sure the settlement money was put away for future needs, sadly some people ignore this. Somehow the money would burn a hole in their pockets and they would buy a new car. The sad thing is that it happened more than once and they wouldn't think to insure the car. And yes, you guessed it but it's too late and the money is gone and the car is written off and they have nothing in reserves for the days off work or the treatment they need.

Confidentiality

When a case is settled out of court, quite often the terms are confidential, meaning that you can't tell anyone, except anyone you are legally obliged to tell.

This can really upset some people as they want to let everyone know that the wrongdoer had to pay and justice was served, so to speak. They end up feeling deprived of their chance to let everyone know that they were in the right and the other party was wrong.

My personal view is that it is best to keep these things private. You don't want people knowing that you are receiving money or how much money you have. That is your business and nobody else's.

And of course, despite giving people advice to keep a settlement private, that would on occasion be ignored. Invariably they would end up ringing me with a new problem of people coming out of the woodwork and chasing old debts or spreading the word of the settlement to others. They would plead: "But I only told a few good friends", and that my friends, is all it takes.

Keep your mouth shut!

A new start

Finalising a claim can mark the time for a fresh start. That chapter is over and while it was no doubt a difficult time, what might have seemed like the worst days of your life are in the past now and you got through it! You have likely learned or practiced persistence and patience. I hope that you can see that if you can navigate that time and experience, you can do anything that you put your mind to.

A case coming to a conclusion is often a huge relief and can lift a weight from a claimant's shoulders. While understanding and accepting that you have made a decision and being able to now be future focussed is a wonderful thing.

Essential points – Chapter 9

- Understanding why you have made a decision to settle or not is very important and it will save you second guessing down the track.
- A case concluding, often brings a sense of relief and overall improvement in well-being.
- The terms of settlement are often confidential so your lawyer can advise you on the specifics of your case. Regardless, I think your personal financial information is best kept confidential.
- Lawyers aren't going to be asking you to look back and talk about the accident and its impacts anymore. This is the time to be future focussed!

Real-life stories

Shirley

Footloose and fancy free! That was me. I had just returned from an overseas trip, and I was planning a road trip around Australia. In three weeks' time I had someone to rent the house and I would set off on the next adventure, or so I thought.

Eleven years ago while I was returning home from the shops, I was on a pedestrian crossing and a car hit me. I sustained injuries after hitting the bonnet, the windscreen and the road. I was in absolute shock, and I didn't realise that at the time. An ambulance came to the scene, and everyone was surprised because there were no major, obvious injuries.

The next day I woke up in pain, bruised and had a very sore hip, which is something that has caused issues to this day. The treatment was to apply heat to my hip. At this stage I thought this was all manageable until the hot water bottle burst, and I suffered second degree burns to my upper thighs and body. I was treated in the burns unit at the hospital and my real recovery started after this.

At this point, I realised that I was not going to travel as I had planned to. However, I was now homeless because my house was rented out and I could not alter the agreement. I had given my furniture to my cousin, and I couldn't work because of the burns.

Fear was really setting in at this time. I became frightened in many respects and simple things like traveling by train became a really difficult and frightening for me.

My close family lived overseas. Dad has a cousin in Australia, so he rang her, and she recommended that I should get a lawyer and passed on details of someone to call. I wasn't looking to make a claim. I was still in shock and my mindset was that I was just lucky to be alive and I should just be thanking my lucky stars. I was encouraged to look beyond that and look to my future and future needs.

The fact that the lawyer had been recommended and I didn't know any different was enough for me. I was so nervous when I went to talk to the lawyer for the first time. I was worried about what he would ask, what I could say and not say and what was expected of me.

The lawyer was great. He led everything and talked me through the process. He clearly had experience in this area and was good at what he did. I understood that I wasn't like him because I didn't have his experience. I was happy for him to take the lead and leave the dotting the i's and crossing the t's to him.

I wanted to stay in Australia. But emotionally I needed more support, so I returned to New Zealand to my family home.

The lawyers told me right from the start that in my circumstances, it would be at least two years to get to a point where we could consider settling the case. The lawyer explained that they would need that sort of time frame to gauge the extent of the injuries and the impact on me in the long term. I had no expectations beyond that.

I found the insurance company frustrating. They required me to attend medical appointments in Australia, three weeks apart, which required me to leave a job in New Zealand. I felt like they were trying to make it difficult for me at the time.

Being overseas and having a lawyer in Australia was no issue. We used email and kept in touch. I felt like I had good rapport with the lawyer and trusted him, so I was pretty relaxed about it all. I was comfortable with the lawyer and may have even cried a few times.

I never felt worried about the claim and about the fact that I was making a claim. In that moment, I was too busy trying to recover, finding a job and a home and I was focussed on just surviving.

Towards the end of the two years, I got on a plane and travelled overseas. At that point of my life, I felt so frightened of everything. My mum encouraged me to get on a plane and remind myself what living and life was about. I was terrified but I got on that plane. I had to be back in Brisbane by a certain date to talk about settling the claim.

I could see early on that the unhealthiest place for me was reliving the experience and going over it. Pouring over documents about it was not going to help. I was so happy to hand that over to the lawyer. I needed to focus my own mind in a place of growth.

We were able to reach an out of court settlement. The lawyer recommended that I accept the insurer's offer and I was accepting of his advice.

The day it was settled and that feeling of being finished is the day I truly started to get better. It wasn't the money that allowed me to get better, but it was being able to let go and not talk about it in that light again. When you are talking to the lawyers and the doctors, you have to talk about the trauma, and how it feels and what you can't do and how that impacts you. Once it was over, I didn't have to have those conversations again.

Eleven years on my life looks much different now. I am a mum to three gorgeous children and run my own online business. What was such a big part of my life at the time is a memory now and I had to charge my memory for the finer details of what happened to share with you here.

My top tips for someone who is injured and looking to make a claim are:

- Find a lawyer you feel that you can trust.
- Put the trust in them and let them run the claim. Mentally and emotionally, you will be better if you can leave it to them and remove yourself from the process.
- You don't know what life will look like in 10 years, so it is important to look into the claims process now.

Peter

My pushbike wasn't just for exercise on a weekend. It was my mode of transport while I studied at university. Being in my early 20s and invincible, I never anticipated that anything bad could happen while riding my bike and minding my own business.

Totally unexpectedly, one early evening, I met the windscreen of a car who failed to give way to me on a roundabout. I was transported to the nearest hospital by ambulance and my actual memory of this time is vague.

I had suffered facial fractures, a closed brain injury and other soft tissue injuries. The road to recovery was my focus and was a long one.

I was supporting myself through university and I was no longer able to work my casual job at the local supermarket. A few concerned friends and family suggested that I contact a lawyer. I was so concerned that it would cost me money that I didn't have, so I didn't initially make a call to a lawyer. My main focus was hospital visits, medical treatment and liaising with the university about how I could defer my studies for the foreseeable future.

I was frightened at receiving a letter from an insurance company demanding I pay for damage to the car that hit me! I had no money, I was injured, and I had a long road to recovery and absolutely no way to pay the demand. This was the catalyst for me contacting a lawyer who then advised me not only did I not have to pay the demand, but it was the insurer that should be compensating me! Steps were taken to lodge a claim on my behalf.

The lawyer that I engaged was recommended by a family friend. I didn't look beyond that and google didn't exist, so there was no way to search reviews. I trusted them based on a recommendation and I was exhausted at this time and so stressed at being sued by the insurance company for damage to the car and I was just relieved that this firm said they would help me and I didn't have to pay upfront.

The lawyer's style was quite aggressive. I never felt like it was good to call him and ask questions. It really felt like a case of: "Don't call me, I'll call you". His letters were quite rude and in one letter he made his typist write an apology for an error in a previous letter. Her apology was something along the lines of: "I am sorry for the error in our previous letter, I am completely incompetent at my job". I later found out that lawyer was struck off and is no longer able to work as a lawyer.

Since then I have had another firm look over the claim and the advice given to me and the result was sound, so while the experience could have been more pleasant, they did a good job.

As a young guy with no money and no job and having signed documents for the firm to represent me, I felt like I had no option but to stick with them. With the benefit of hindsight and experience it was probably warranted to take my file to a lawyer who I felt I had a good rapport with, but in saying that the end result was satisfactory.

The claims process seemed to go forever. If the lawyer had advised me upfront that it would take a number of years, I think I would have felt less frustrated. Every time I thought that we had everything we needed to resolve the claim, I would be required to go to another specialist appointment for a medical report to be used in the claim.

This was stressful, because I would see their invoices and I had no idea how these reports would be paid for. I also felt like I had to tell my story over and over. This was tiring, and I don't think I understood it at this time, but it wasn't helpful to my recovery to be going over what happened, the injury and what I could no longer do.

The point came where my legal team and I met with the insurer, and we were able to come to an out of court settlement. This was an utter sense of relief for me. My injuries had stabilised, I was back at university, I had been so concerned that I'd end up owing the lawyer money, so to have a situation where I received some compensation, and the lawyers were paid was a massive relief. I felt like that chapter could be closed and I could move on.

Since then, I was able to graduate from university and work in the information technology industry. I worked up the nerve to get on my bike again and enjoy riding to this day. Now, I prefer the trails to the road. If I was to tell a colleague about the accident, I think they would be genuinely surprised to learn about it. It was such a massive part of my life for a few years, but now it really is a distant memory.

My top tips for someone who is injured and looking to make a claim are:

- Understand the timeline. If the lawyer doesn't advise you on this, ask. This way you will have reasonable expectations around time and feel less frustration.
- Engage a lawyer who you have good rapport with, and you feel you can ask questions to.
- Don't ring the lawyer unnecessarily! They charge fees every time that you call.
- Understand the costs agreement. It will save you unnecessary worries over the unknown.
- If you get a sense that something is not good with your lawyer, don't be afraid to seek a second opinion or escalate it to a supervisor in the firm.

Ruby-Lee

As someone working in a law firm, you don't imagine yourself being the client.

When I was involved in a motor vehicle accident, I was working in a law firm as a clerk and studying Justice Studies at university. It wasn't a highly paid job and I had just bought a house. I was in my 20s and single. The mortgage and living expenses were my sole responsibility.

I was on my way to work, driving my Hyundai Excel and was hit from behind by a truck. Ironically, this happened outside a hospital. The car was hit with some force and my head hit the door frame. I initially thought I was okay and went to work. About an hour after arriving at work, probably when the adrenaline wore off, I collapsed at my desk.

It was the week before Christmas and a busy time in the office and add to that the fact I felt stressed about being solely responsible for the mortgage and taking time off work really worried me.

Because I was travelling to work when I was injured, I was able to organise some WorkCover benefits to help with treatment costs and time off work. In hindsight, I should have taken more time off to rest and recover. I suffered an injury to my neck and shoulder. One rib became displaced, and I was diagnosed with traffic phobia.

The firm I worked for was representing me and lodged the claim. I was familiar with the claims process, so I didn't give it much thought in terms of getting them to represent me and lodge the claim.

Through WorkCover I had multiple scans, a variety of treatment, specialist appointments, exercise physiology and therapy to get me driving again. The pain was exhausting to me. I would come from work to home so tired.

Later, I commenced work for another law firm, and I considered taking my claim there. I was given advice to transfer my file to another firm where I did not work. The people that I worked with, may have been called as witnesses to give evidence about my capacity to work and the impact of the injuries on my work. They couldn't act for me and be called as witnesses, so it made sense to have a separate firm act for me. Then I was represented by a firm who had experience in similar claims acting for professionals.

I quickly built rapport with the new lawyer. It helped that I knew the claims process and generally what to expect. I was conscious not to call them all the time with trivial things because I knew that would just inflate the fees. We communicated a lot by email as that suited me.

I never considered acting for myself. What's the saying? The lawyer that represents themselves has a fool for a client! There is an emotional toll of retelling the story especially when you are already in pain and tired. Also, there is the burden of administration, time limits etc. The time I did have, I thought was better used going to medical treatment etc. I think having someone independent act for me meant that I didn't have to think about it all so much.

After the accident, I decided to further my studies and study law and become properly qualified as a lawyer. There were concerns that I would not be able to complete the studies because of the injuries, so the advice was to hold off on settling the claim until we knew whether I'd cope with the studies and the workload as a lawyer.

When it came time to discuss a possible settlement, I was familiar with the process, but I trusted my legal team, the lawyer and the barrister. I found the process difficult in that I felt like the insurer and their team didn't believe me and thought that I was out to play the system. As a young lawyer, my reputation was everything and I found it hard to think that they didn't believe me. Having my team there, that I really trusted, helped me that day.

The settlement was a relief in that I didn't have to worry about lawyers, insurers and doctors not believing me.

Regarding the length of time to settle my claim, it was definitely considered on the longer side. My legal team had explained why we should not rush to try to settle. They wanted to see if I could finish my studies and if I could cope with workload as a lawyer. I trusted their advice and I understood why the claim couldn't settle sooner rather than later. I might not have liked that advice, but I understood and accepted it.

I would have friends asking me "haven't you settled yet, my friend's claim settled ages ago". Luckily, I understood why the claim was taking longer than average to settle and I knew not to get caught up in what other people were saying. It would have been really stressful if had have worried every time someone told me about their friend's claim not taking as long.

Many years have passed since this time. At 6-12 months post-accident, I was starting to really worry and question if I was ever going to get better and thinking how no amount of money was going to make it better. Years later though, I did finish my law degree, I was able to become admitted as a lawyer, and I am now self-employed, and I run my own law firm.

When my injuries play up, I am able to manage my own time around that. I have a mindset to get on with things which helps. I found it's important to let people know that I have injuries that play up, and because of that people understand me better and I find they relate to me better too. Life certainly didn't stop for me after the accident. I was able to still achieve so much and keep going, even though it didn't always feel that way.

My tips for anyone considering or making a claim are:

- Get advice from a personal injury lawyer on your specific situation. In terms of finding a lawyer for a referral, do you know someone who had a claim? Who acted for them?
- Get properly diagnosed, you know your body better. If you think there is something wrong, get a medical opinion and a second one if needed.
- Don't call your lawyer just for a chat because you are only inflating your own fees. Give your lawyer exactly what you are being asked for.
- Where you can, keep records of receipts, so your lawyer isn't wading through bundles of receipts that have faded over time.
- Trust the lawyer and trust that they know what they are doing.
- If something hasn't been explained to you to a level you understand, ask!
- Don't be taking legal advice from your friends because your friends aren't lawyers.

Cindy

Thirty years of accident-free driving came to an end in one day, with not one accident, but two!

I was sitting stationary at a set of lights when a distracted driver hit her accelerator and launched into my small car. I immediately felt neck pain and my arm was numb. I have never been in a car accident or suffered injuries like this and I don't think I realised how serious it was. I went home and took some Nurofen, and fully expected to recover without issues.

The next day, on Christmas Eve, I had an appointment to go to and while I didn't feel great, I didn't want to cancel at short notice. While driving to that appointment, a car turned and collided with the passenger side of my vehicle. I couldn't believe it. Two accidents in less than 24 hours! I suffered instant pain in my neck and even though I had never had it before, I thought to myself, this must be whiplash.

I consulted my GP straight away. The doctor prescribed medication for nerve damage and referred me for scans and x-rays. I took pain medication and I really believed I'd return to my pre accident health. Having never suffered neck or back pain, I think I was quite naive.

On New Year's Eve, a friend mentioned that I should get a lawyer. I hadn't even considered it until then. I didn't realise that would be available for me in that situation. My friend made a recommendation for a lawyer to contact.

I contacted the lawyer that was recommended to me. Because he came on a recommendation, I had no hesitations, and I did not shop around. He was a specialist insurance claims lawyer, so I didn't really question the decision to engage him. It never occurred to me that some lawyers might be better than others or that their terms would vary.

At this time I was working in consulting on an information technology project. I felt I had to keep going because there was a mortgage and school fees to pay. As it was the holiday season, I had time off through to February.

I met the lawyer once and the remainder of our communication was by phone and email. Unfortunately, I later learned that he was hopelessly disorganised. I was constantly chasing him for updates because I never knew what was happening or what the next steps were. I would let it go for long periods and months at a time, but it was always up to me to contact him to find out what was happening.

He was never available to take my calls, which I understand because he has other clients and meetings etc. However, it would always take at least a week to return to my call and he could never tell me what was happening. He would always give me lame excuses like:

"I haven't heard", "I need to chase". I felt like it was all delay tactics to get him more time. There was never anything proactive about his actions.

I was never provided with advice on the process and associated timelines. On reflection, I wish I knew to ask for that. That would have saved me always ringing to find out what was happening and would have held the lawyer to that timeline too.

I did consider finding a new lawyer to represent me, but I kept thinking that we must be close to ending this claim soon.

Three and a half years after the accidents, my claim settled. That was a strange process. I felt like the lawyer and barrister knew all the processes and it was routine for them, but they forgot to tell me what was going on and what to expect.

Settling the claim brought a huge sense of relief, until then it felt like the claims were hanging over my head. The endless going over the details and talking about pain feels like you aren't moving on and feels like you are wallowing. I wanted to move forward in my life. Settling the claim did give that sense that I could move on.

There was a sense of guilt in taking the money. I have never been given money in a lump sum like that before. I felt very grateful and knew that I had to use it wisely.

Real-life stories

My tips for anyone considering or making a claim are:

- Find a good lawyer!
- Make sure your lawyer explains the process and timelines, so you know what it is happening and what to expect.
- If you feel something isn't right with the lawyer, ask questions and don't be afraid to ask for a second opinion.
- Keep chasing your lawyer if they aren't responding. It is a red flag if they are not responding to you.

Anastasia

What should have been a celebration, ended up being one of the most traumatic experiences of my life. I was leaving an end of year work event and awards night and was helping my boss carry some things to the car. When I was walking down the stairs, my heel became caught in a faulty tread on the step, and I fell knees first down the flight of stairs. The good news was I didn't drop anything in the spectacular fall! The bad news was that my shin was grated down every one of the metal treads on the steps.

The injury was serious, my shin was cut deeply from my knee to my ankle. My team were fantastic at coming to my aid and an ambulance was called. The venue were quite unhelpful and it was only at our insistence that an accident report was completed, albeit a poorly completed one. I was at the hospital until early the next morning where I received treatment. The wound was cleaned and stitched, and I was sent home to recover.

The pain of this injury was insane. I suffered pain and medication induced nausea and vomiting. Each time the medical team came to look at it and touch the bandages, the pain was unbelievable. I was previously involved in a head on collision, and this was right up there in terms of how traumatic it was.

We were due to take a family vacation to Byron Bay just after the accident. We still went, but it was the most depressing holiday for me. I couldn't get my leg wet. I was in a lot of pain and I sat while everyone went and enjoyed the holiday. It was beautiful but depressing at the same time.

At this time, I was running my own business, as well working as a marriage celebrant and doing part time work in digital marketing for a local business. Also, I am a mum of two primary school girls. After the accident, there was a period of time where I just couldn't work. I couldn't drive my girls anywhere. It was school holidays, so we couldn't fully enjoy that like we normally would.

Initially, I had to go to the local GP every day for the wound to be tended to, that was then every second day and finally every third day. These visits to the GP went on for two months. This meant that I had to find someone who could drive me there. I found this so hard. I am extremely independent, and I don't like asking for help. I felt like I was always asking for favours and like I was a big inconvenience to everyone including the doctor.

The venue dealt with the entire situation poorly. From us insisting that the manager make an incident report to ringing the next day, and speaking to my husband, to say they understood a terrible thing happened and to offer me a free dinner, there was no apology, no asking how I was. In that conversation they referred to seeing video footage of me fall. My husband asked to see the footage they referred to and he was advised that it was an insurance company policy that wouldn't allow him to see it, but instead offered the details of their insurer if I want to make a claim.

My manager had mentioned that she had suffered an injury in an accident years before, and never did anything about it. She said that she now regrets that she didn't pursue compensation and encouraged me to consider that.

I never thought I'd be bringing a claim for compensation, but the conversation with my manager, the fact that the venue gave us their insurance details and imagining all the other vulnerable people who would encounter those stairs nudged me to make an enquiry with a lawyer.

We had a friend who had worked in law, so I asked her for a recommendation for a lawyer who might be able to help me. I met with the lawyer, and I felt confused at first if it was something I should pursue. The lawyer acknowledged that it was no doubt traumatic but said that we needed to prove fault on the part of the venue. The lawyer advised me that we should start the process and see what the venue and their insurers say.

My concerns were that I'd end up owing money or that I'd go through all this and all the money would go to the lawyer. I understood that the lawyer couldn't promise an outcome, but I didn't want to waste his time or mine.

It surprised me that I was worried about the stigma of being a personal injury claimant. I found that socially, I was justifying why I was making a claim by explaining that I was in pain, that the stairs needed to be fixed and that I didn't want to regret not doing something down the track.

My lawyers organised for me to see a medical specialist who wrote a medical report as part of my claim. I felt like that process and the report really helped. As much as I am a positive person, that was the one time I felt it was important to say it how it was. I think we have a tendency to play things down and say: "I'll be right", but I read over my diary notes, especially those first few months after the accident and I told the doctor what it was really like and how bad the pain was.

Eighteen months after the accident we were able to settle the claim. It was a relief to have it settled. I was able to pay the lawyer and have the compensation to help me in the future as I need it. It was a terrible thing that happened, but I feel that my lawyer secured a good outcome for me. Having the claim over, meant that I could go on in a positive way and there was definitely a sense of closure.

Almost three years later, while the injury can still play up, it's actually hard to remember all the details. But I'm not bitter and jaded about it because I was compensated, and I focus on what I have to be happy about.

Interestingly the venue was renovated and the last thing that they did a month after my claim settled was to resurface the stairs with a proper edge.

My tips for anyone considering or making a claim are:

- Take photos. It was so helpful to explain what happened because I had photos from the night that my team thought to take.
- Keep notes. You think you'll remember everything, but you don't. I kept notes on when I went to the doctor, when I needed help, who drove me, things I missed out on and how I felt. Without the notes it would be in my nature to make things not as bad as they were.
- Trust the process. My lawyer said he'd take care of it so I had to trust that it wasn't his first case and that he knew what he was doing.
- Know that it will all work out in the end.

Conclusion

An accident, an injury, the associated losses and then having to deal with lawyers really can be a lot for anyone to deal with. In such a time of uncertainty, an injured person really can be left feeling overwhelmed, not knowing where to start and second guessing themselves.

My hope is that you will find some peace of mind here. It is not possible for me to physically be there for you and hold your hand through the process, but through this book I hope you have found some answers, felt reassured and could sleep easier. I have addressed what were the recurring questions and concerns that I saw as a personal injury lawyer over my career.

I recommend keeping this book within reach and referring back to chapters as you reach those stages of your claim. What you read may well just reinforce what your lawyer is telling you and what is happening. Or perhaps it will confirm for you that something happening is a red flag and it's time to ask questions.

Communication is everything and when I look back on cases where clients were dissatisfied or frustrated, it almost always could be attributed to a lack of clear communication. You can't control the communication style or frequency of an individual lawyer or firm, but you can ask questions. It is better for you to send an email or pick up the phone and ask a question than allow it to build up in your mind and often become a bigger issue than it is.

Depending on where you are right now in the process, it can seem like it will never be over and that you are in the worst period of your life. What I can assure you is that this time will pass, even though it might not feel like it right now.

The reason I included the stories which were so generously shared is that they have been through it, just like you, but they are now on the other side. For some of them it was all consuming at the time, and now, they really had to jog their memories to answer my questions. Many have moved on to have amazing life experiences, something they never thought would be possible at the time they were injured. There really is a light at the end of the tunnel!

It is not always possible to speak to someone who has been through something similar so, this was an opportunity to hear from someone that has been through an accident, injury, the uncertainty and the

Conclusion

claims process. I hope that they give you confidence that where you are at right now, will pass.

What I have observed in the stories and in my own experience acting for people over the years is that the ones who went on to enjoy a full life and new experiences were future focussed and weren't defined by what happened. They dealt with it and moved on and it became something that happened years ago.

My wish is that you get through the claims process and feel that you have good rapport and trust with and in your lawyer. And when your claim settles, I hope that your thoughts about the event and the injury end there too and after that you can be focussed on your yet to be written future!

Special people

I honestly thought this book would be so easy and quick to put together. I was wrong!

Without wonderful people around me, this book would not be in your hands.

I am eternally grateful that through education and a full career I was equipped to write this book. This would not have been the reality without some very important people in my life:

- My mum and dad, thank you for your constant encouragement and belief that I could do anything I put my mind to. Thank you!
- A, shall remain nameless, teacher who told me that Queensland University of Technology (QUT) was too fine an establishment for someone like me. That put a fire in my belly and saw me graduate from QUT with business and law degrees. Thank you!
- Richard, you gave me a go as a young, articled clerk. It was a leap of faith on your part and it

was the start of a very rewarding career for me. You also showed me what was possible with hard work. Thank you!

- Andy, you were always there to answer my questions and guide me and help with the really difficult matters while making it a lot of fun and laughs! Without your guidance, I may never have discovered Luntz. Thank you!
- The TML team, what a magic time that was! Being part of that transformation was something special. Thank you!

While I had the idea, the knowledge and experience to bring you this book, I really couldn't have done it without these people around me today:

- Annette, my accountability buddy through lockdowns. Without our weekly Sunday calls those chapters never would have got written. Thank you!
- The team at Gowor International Publishing. You took my work from ideas and notes and helped make it into a reality. Thank you!
- To the people who so generously and vulnerably shared their stories to help you. Thank you!
- Team "Ohana", the belief, encouragement and inspiration you provide is like no other. Without you, the doubts and fears could have taken over

and this book never would have come to be. Thank you!
- Jon, the most patient man alive. Thank you!
- Rupert, you make me want to do and be my best. Thank you!

About The Author

Lisa Rennie is a happily retired and recovering lawyer. With 18 years' experience in personal injury law, working for injured people, Lisa has seen the full range of emotions, fears and concerns from her clients.

Rather than closing the door on that chapter of her life, she has put pen to paper to bring you some reassurance and guidance on working with a lawyer based on her experience and the many conversations she has had with clients over the years.

Lisa enjoyed a rewarding career in law and a highlight was her time as General Manager of one of Queensland's leading personal injury firms.

Now Lisa enjoys her time building online businesses, travel and running a busy household.

Her hope is that this book will encourage greater and more effective communication between lawyers and their clients and save unnecessary angst for all involved.

To contact Lisa, head to lisarennie.com